"A stunningly unique book! With a tone that reads like a conversation between old friends, Bo lays out some simple and witty rules for understanding the difference between being lucky and being smart. A must read for anyone who wants to be more entrepreneurial."

—LARRY WEBER, founder, Weber Shandwick

"*Lucky or Smart* is one of those rare business books that's as fun to read as it is illuminating. By page ten you'll be hankering to start up a new company, and by the end, you'll actually have the tools to do it. It's an essential addition to any entrepreneur's library."

—STEVEN JOHNSON, author of *Emergence and Mind Wide Open*

"Every entrepreneur I meet with will get a copy of *Lucky or Smart?*. It has invaluable insights regarding the relationship between venture capitalists and entrepreneurs."

—PETER BARRIS, managing partner, New Enterprise Associates

"Bo Peabody's firsthand recounting of his experiences as a B-student entrepreneur attracting and motivating A-student managers is a surprisingly accurate portrayal of the qualities needed to supercharge start-up businesses. It gives encouragement and confidence to all of us other B-students to know that success is not all based on academic achievement."

—ALAN PATRICOF, co-founder, Apax Partners

Lucky
or Smart?

RANDOM HOUSE

BUSINESS BOOKS

Lucky
or Smart?

SECRETS

TO AN

ENTREPRENEURIAL

LIFE

Bo Peabody

Published by Random House Business Books in 2005

1 3 5 7 9 10 8 6 4 2

Copyright © 2005 by Peabody Enterprises

Bo Peabody has asserted his right under the Copyright,
Designs and Patents Act, 1988 to be identified as the author
of this work

First published in the United States by Random House,
a division of Random House Inc. in 2005

Random House Business Books
The Random House Group Limited
20 Vauxhall Bridge Road, London SW1V 2SA

Random House Australia (Pty) Limited
20 Alfred Street, Milsons Point, Sydney,
New South Wales 2061, Australia

Random House New Zealand Limited
18 Poland Road, Glenfield
Auckland 10, New Zealand

Random House (Pty) Limited
Endulini, 5a Jubilee Road, Parktown 2193, South Africa

The Random House Group Limited Reg. No. 954009

www.randomhouse.co.uk

businessbooks@randomhouse.co.uk

A CIP catalogue record for this book
is available from the British Library

Papers used by Random House
are natural, recyclable products made from wood grown in
sustainable forests. The manufacturing processes conform to
the environmental regulations of the country of origin

ISBN 1 8441 3691 4

Printed and bound in Great Britain by
Cox & Wyman Ltd, Reading, Berkshire

Dedicated to Nate Kurz,

Tung Pham, Emma Taylor,

and Jeff Vanderclute:

the Unsung Heroes

of Tripod

CONTENTS

INTRODUCTION

My career from ages eighteen to twenty-eight:

- In 1991, as a college freshman, I had an idea for an online service offering "real life" education to college students: practical advice about jobs, personal finance, and health. I made the simple observations that no one was teaching us these subjects in the classroom, and that computers—rather than books or TVs—had become the primary medium of communication and entertainment for my generation.

- During my sophomore year, Dick Sabot, a very smart Oxford-trained Ph.D. in economics and the professor of a class in which I received a B-minus, agreed to collaborate with me on my nascent concept. He did so not because I was his best student, but because he had had a near-death experience during which a higher power advised him to do "something different."

- By 1994, when I graduated from college, our project had indeed become something different: an Internet start-up company we named Tripod. Despite the fact that 99.9 percent of the American public had never even heard of the Internet, I decided to stick with Tripod. I graduated Summa Cum Nada, and it would have been impossible for me to get a decent "real job" with my not-so-decent but very real grades.

- Using what little cash I could raise from friends and family, I hired a team of computer programmers. I did this because

I did not know how to install a web browser on my own computer, which is a significant barrier if you plan to run an Internet company.

- Unbeknownst to me, and surely with some sort of anarchic motive, these lawless, long-haired, multi-pierced, tattooed, incredibly charming and smart hacker hooligans built a piece of software on Tripod that had nothing to do with offering practical advice to anyone. Instead, this software gave individuals the power to publish their own "personal homepages."

- By 1995, the popularity of the Tripod Homepage Builder was growing rapidly and had far surpassed my original idea to offer college students "practical advice." It occurred to me that I might have a business on my hands. Having never written a business plan, I went to the local library and checked out a book called—you guessed it—*How to Write a Business Plan*.

- In August 1995, Netscape went public and proved that Internet companies had value. Or at least proved that Wall Street investment bankers had convinced the stock-buying public that Internet companies had value.

- One month later, I was able to convince New Enterprise Associates (NEA), one of the world's most respected venture capital firms, to review the Tripod business plan. They agreed to do so only because Dick's wife's brother's college roommate knew someone who knew someone at NEA.

- NEA liked the plan because it mentioned the Internet several hundred times.

- In November 1995, Tripod received $3 million in financing from NEA.

- I based Tripod in Williamstown, a six-thousand-person

college town in the mountains of northwestern Massachusetts, not because it made much business sense, but because I really like to ski.

- Given the media frenzy in the late nineties surrounding "kids" and their "cool" Internet start-ups, the decision to locate in Williamstown resulted in thousands of newspaper articles, magazine stories, TV clips, and radio interviews about Tripod, most of which featured me either riding my mountain bike to work or using the word "dude." The former of which I actually did only the half a dozen times my 1983 shit-box Volkswagen Rabbit was in the shop. The latter of which I still do.

- By the beginning of 1996, one year after it was launched, the Tripod Homepage Builder had fundamentally changed the nature of consumer media. For the first time, anyone with access to a computer and a connection to the Internet could publish pretty much whatever they wanted; and anyone else with access to a computer and a connection to the Internet could view it.

- By the middle of 1997, Tripod had attracted nearly one million registered members.

- Tripod never posted a profit.

- Tripod generated barely any revenue.

- On December 30, 1997, in the middle of the stock-market bubble, I was offered $58 million for Tripod.

- On December 31, 1997, I agreed to sell Tripod in exchange for $58 million in stock of a publicly traded company named Lycos, which at the time was an Internet company only slightly more stable than Tripod.

- I agreed to a "lockup" that forbade me to sell all of my Lycos stock for two years.

- Over those two years, I watched the value of my Lycos stock increase tenfold.
- By December 31, 1999, at the height of the bubble and just a few months before the market crashed, I had sold nearly every share of my Lycos stock.
- I invested the majority of those proceeds in bonds and real estate because they were the only two investment vehicles I could thoroughly understand. And because I needed a house.

When all this happens to you, and certainly when it happens to you before you turn twenty-eight years old, you can be sure of one thing: Forever, often and always, you will be asked that loaded question, "Were you lucky or were you smart?"

In response, most people immediately give a two-part answer: They recite the trite adage "I'd rather be lucky than smart," and then they sigh and say, "Well, you know, it was a little of both."

I give a different answer:

"I was smart enough to realize I was getting lucky."

And that's the right answer. It might in fact be the only completely right answer I've ever given. Hey, even a blind squirrel finds a nut sometimes.

Over the past decade, through the bubble and the burst, I have co-founded six companies, all of which have survived, if not done fairly well. Along the way, I've learned some things that may be useful, but perhaps not obvious, to someone thinking of starting his or her own business. What follows are some simple observations that may help entrepreneurs get a little lucky, and therefore more successfully navigate the start-up process.

Lucky
or Smart?

1.

Lucky or Smart?

Luck is a part of life, and everyone, at one point or another, gets lucky. But luck is a *big* part of business life and perhaps the *biggest* part of entrepreneurial life. At the very least, entrepreneurs must believe in luck. Ideally, they can recognize it when they see it. And over time, the best entrepreneurs can actually learn to create luck.

Luck in business is different from regular old luck, like when you find $20 on the sidewalk. First of all, "being lucky" in business has an intoxicating underbelly called "being smart." No one actually believes that he should take credit for finding $20 on the sidewalk. But when people get lucky in business, they are often convinced that it is not luck at all that brought them good fortune. They believe instead that their business venture succeeded thanks to their own blinding brilliance. The number-one killer of start-ups is when entrepreneurs confuse "being lucky" with "being smart." You must possess the humility to distinguish one from the other.

The big challenge is that everyone—the press, your shareholders, your colleagues, your significant other, and your parents—will work hard to convince you otherwise. They will tell you, over and over again, that you are in fact a genius and should take complete credit for all the great things happening to your company. Why? Because to them, you are one of the following:

1. *A source of professional gain*
2. *A source of financial gain*
3. *Their boss*
4. *Their lover*
5. *Their pride and joy*

None of these relationships provide any incentive for any of these people to tell you the cold hard truth about your entrepreneurial success: You may have gotten just plain lucky.

The second difference between "business luck" and "everyday luck" is that luck in business can be created, whereas everyday luck cannot. You can't will yourself to find $20 on the sidewalk. But you can create a company that gets lucky more often than your average company. Indeed, there is a pseudo-scientific formula for creating business luck. And the key element is this: Lucky things happen to entrepreneurs who start fundamentally innovative, morally compelling, and philosophically positive companies.

Why? Because lots of smart people will gather around companies with these qualities. As it turns out, precious few of them exist. And the vast majority of human beings, and certainly most of the smart ones, are constitutionally caring creatures who would, if given the chance, prefer to spend their valuable time in a positive setting contributing to the betterment of society rather than in a negative setting contributing to its detriment. Shocking, I know, but true.

And when smart, inspired people gather around a fundamentally innovative, morally compelling, and philosophically positive company, they work very hard. And when smart, inspired people work very hard, serendipity ensues. Serendipity—the faculty of making fortuitous discoveries by chance—causes lots of unexpected things to happen to a company. Some of these unexpected things are good. Some are bad. But because no one planned for the good things to happen, they appear as luck. In other words, the best way to ensure that lucky things happen is to make sure that a lot of things happen. It's really that simple.

In applying this formula, the entrepreneur has two tasks:

1. *Create an environment where*
   smart people will gather.
   and
2. *Be smart enough to stay out of the way*
   and let luck happen.

5

Good entrepreneurs are not, per se, lucky or smart. They are just smart enough to realize when they are getting lucky. It's a subtle but very important distinction.

Of course, there are entrepreneurs who start fundamentally silly, morally bankrupt, and philosophically negative companies. These entrepreneurs and their ventures fail more for lack of luck than for any lack of raw entrepreneurial skills. These destined-to-self-destruct companies are, first and foremost, about the entrepreneur trying to make a million dollars rather than about doing anything interesting or valuable. As a result, these companies don't attract the smart people who generate luck.

Much of what makes a company fundamentally innovative, morally compelling, and philosophically positive is not what the company's business model actually is, but how the entrepreneur communicates the mission of the company. A company's mission, communicated by the entrepreneur with charisma and passion, is what creates the environment that attracts smart people and gets them inspired in the first place. Which is exactly what gets the luck rolling.

Tripod made what money it did by selling advertising to clients such as Ford and Visa. That was our business model. But Tripod's mission, as I described it to my colleagues, was to revolutionize consumer media, allowing anyone to publish his or her views to the entire world using the Tripod Homepage Builder. Suddenly, almost overnight, the stories, viewpoints, and opinions of every individual, interest group, or culture could be made available for others to grapple with. "Tripod isn't here just to make money," I told my colleagues. "We are here to fight the most important battles on the frontier of the First Amendment!"

6   Mezze, the restaurant group I later co-founded in the Berkshire Hills of Massachusetts, serves food and drink to locals and to tourists from New York City and Boston. That's our business model. But the mission of Mezze is larger: to set an example of quality and service for all the Berkshires' retail establishments. I tell our staff that by working hard to refine Mezze, we raise the bar for everyone. And that by doing so, we will together attract more visitors to our small part of the world.

Village Ventures, the venture capital firm I co-founded in 2000, makes money by taking advantage of the supply and demand imbalance that results from the concentration of venture capital in only a few large cities. That's our business model. But the mission of Village Ventures is different: to enable entrepreneurs to start companies in the towns where they want to live. Rather than having to flee to Boston or San Francisco to find venture capital, entrepreneurs in Boise, Idaho, and Providence, Rhode Island, can get capital from Village Ventures right in their own hometowns and build their companies in the same place they'd like to raise their families.

Missions such as those of Tripod, Mezze, and Village Ventures create an "aura of authenticity," which is the elixir that attracts smart people and inspires them. Authenticity is an adjective rarely used to describe anything in the modern business world. But it's just the thing that people crave most in their work. And there is nothing more authentic in business than a fundamentally innovative, morally compelling, and philosophically positive company whose mission has been crafted carefully and communicated with charisma and passion. That's because the primary goal of these companies is not to make money but to defend the First Amendment and create jobs in places where there aren't many. And people love that. No matter what anyone might tell you, all but the most hardened human beings want to believe that they get up in the morning to pursue a goal greater than simply padding their pockets.

But the Holy Grail of business is making money doing something you really believe in. So when people find themselves aboard one of these vessels, they don't want to get off. They form a fierce protective boundary around it and will do anything to keep the vessel afloat and its inhabitants alive. These people are liberated by finding not only a way to make money but also a way to feel good about it. This is what takes inspiration and turns it into hard work. And the results of smart people working hard are serendipity and luck.

My formula for getting lucky in business is reasonably simple: Start a company that is fundamentally innovative, morally compelling, and philosophically positive. Create an aura of authenticity around your start-up by carefully crafting your mission and communicating it with charisma and passion. Your company will quickly attract smart, inspired people who will work very hard. Treat all these people fairly. Provide them with a clear action plan and give them the latitude to exercise their creativity. The results: serendipity, luck, success, and, ultimately, money. And the only smart thing about this formula is that on a day-to-day basis *my* brain has very little to do with any of it.

2.

Entrepreneurs Are Born, Not Made

In 1998, the persona of the "entrepreneur"—a relatively young term, coined only 150 years ago—skyrocketed into the global consciousness. Thanks in large part to companies like Ebay and Yahoo!, kids that previously would have aspired to become astronauts and doctors now wanted to be Internet entrepreneurs. At the same time, thanks to countless cable-television shows, the persona of the celebrity chef and restaurant owner—or "restaurateurs," as they are called—was likewise capturing the imagination of the American psyche. Irrespective of the industry, starting your own business was suddenly very hip.

When I was growing up, "entrepreneur" carried roughly the same connotation as "inventor." The word conjured images of your wacky uncle doing science experiments in his basement in search of a new species of peanut butter. But by the late nineties, "entrepreneur" meant millionaire and celebrity. And that meant that everyone wanted to be an entrepreneur. The problem is this: Very few people *are* entrepreneurs.

People often ask me, "When did you decide to become an entrepreneur?" I never decided to be an entrepreneur. It just happened. I started mowing lawns when I was ten. I moved to snow-blowing the driveways next to those lawns when I was thirteen. And finally on to sealcoating (sealcoat is a sticky, tarlike substance used to preserve pavement) those same driveways when I was sixteen. My logic: I had the customers, and the more distasteful, dirty, and degrading a task it was to maintain a square foot of their property, the more they were willing to pay me to do it. Pretty simple.

Entrepreneurs are born, not made. One does not decide to be an entrepreneur. One *is* an entrepreneur. Those who *decide* to become entrepreneurs are making the first in a long line of bad business decisions.

The most egregious example of people deciding to be entrepreneurs takes place in the restaurant business. The conventional wisdom is that anyone who can cook can open a restaurant. Simply add a few attractive college students to serve your yummy fare to the horde of salivating customers waiting at your door on opening night, and boom: Just like that, you're in the restaurant business. Ironically, despite the fact that this is indeed the conventional wisdom, when I tell people that I'm in the restaurant business, they always say the same thing: "Wow, that's a tough business."

The truth is, both statements are correct: Anyone who can cook can open a restaurant, and it is a tough business. Indeed, the restaurant business is a tough business precisely because anyone can open a restaurant. Let me explain.

The restaurant business, as businesses go, is not difficult to understand and analyze. In fact, it's quite easy. It's one of the few businesses in which you get near-perfect data every single day on your customers' likes and dislikes. If the customers like the scallops, leave them on the menu. If they don't, take them off. If the customers tip the waiter well, continue to employ him. If they don't, let him go. Pretty simple. Gathering and preparing food are the most basic tasks of humans. When we outsource those tasks, we are, like hungry infants, in a vulnerable and difficult-to-please state. Restaurant-goers are, therefore, not shy. They are all too happy to tell you what they think, and invariably, they vote with their wallets.

Compare this to the software business, where it might take two years to get a product ready for market and then another year to make the first sale. Only then, more than three years later, after your customers have been using the product for a few months in an actual business setting, will you know what they really think. Thankfully, using software is not a human's most basic task. But for collecting feedback on a product, I'll take the scallop situation any day.

When people say "The restaurant business is a tough business," what they mean to say is "A lot of restaurants fail." This is entirely correct. Four out of five restaurants fail, but not because the restaurant business is a tough business. It's because four out of five people who open restaurants shouldn't be in the restaurant business at all. These people follow the conventional wisdom that anyone can start a restaurant, and they get into the business for all the wrong reasons:

1. *They like food and know more about it than the average sustenance-driven slob.*
2. *They like to cook for friends. And these same friends have always told them, "You know, you should really think about opening a restaurant."*

3. *They want more friends, and giving away free food is a great way to get more friends.*
4. *They like to be the center of attention.*
5. *They've always wanted to design a restaurant.*

None of these things have anything to do with actually running a restaurant: necessary tasks such as negotiating a lease, bringing a building up to code, obtaining a liquor license, managing inventory, and motivating staff. All this, however, never stops these would-be restaurateurs. These unfortunate folk have decided that they are going to be entrepreneurs, rather than trying to understand whether or not they actually are entrepreneurs. This is why four out of five restaurants fail.

It may not be immediately apparent to you whether you are or aren't an entrepreneur. Just because you never had a lemonade stand doesn't mean you won't be the next Bill Gates or Emeril Lagasse. And just because you hawked some sugar water to the nice old lady next door doesn't mean you will be.

Here is a simple multiple-choice question to help you assess your entrepreneurial aptitude:

When you look up at a cloud, which of the following best describes your thoughts?

A. *Wow, that cloud would make a great painting.*
B. *Hmmm, how would I describe that cloud to someone else?*
C. *What a silly question. I never look up at clouds.*
D. *Let's see. I wonder if I could manufacture an environmentally friendly chemical that instantaneously*

creates or dissolves clouds within a perfectly defined geographical area?

E. *Gee, I wonder exactly how a cloud is formed.*

If you answered A, good luck with your career as a painter, graphic designer, floral arranger, architect, interior decorator, or makeup artist. You are aesthetically minded. Starting a company will just corrupt that very positive quality.

If you answered B, good luck in your profession as a writer or a teacher. We need more people like you. But we don't need more people like you starting companies.

If you answered C, good luck at basic training. You have no time for cloud-gazing. The military is a good place for you to exercise your extraordinary focus.

If you answered D, go directly to chapter 3. You are most likely an entrepreneur.

If you answered E, read on. There is still hope.

In the business world, answering E is as good as answering D. You may not be an entrepreneur, or even entrepreneurial, but you most likely have a knack for managing a business. You are interested in fully understanding the details: What are clouds? What substances are they made up of? What causes them to appear? What causes them to disappear? You'd be a great chemist in my little make-believe start-up, managing the team of chemists that will discover that revolutionary, environmentally friendly chemical. Or you might be the lawyer that will help sort through the patent and Department of Environmental Protection issues. You could also be the sales-and-marketing professional who gets excited by the intricacies of the product rollout plans, the channel distribution strategies, and the inevitable customer-service challenges.

If you answered E, chances are you are a manager, not an entrepreneur. You should go to a training program at an investment bank like Morgan Stanley, or to a management-consulting firm like Bain. You should then go and spend three or four years working inside a big company. You might then consider attending law school or maybe even medical school. At some point, you should certainly go to business school. You should do whatever you can to expose yourself to the best practices and classical training of the business world.

But don't start a business. You will most likely fail. Not because you aren't smart but because you are *too* smart.

3.

Entrepreneurs Are B-Students.
Managers Are A-Students.

My mom used to always say, "Bo, you could go to Harvard or to the local community college; no matter what, you'll always get a B."

Mom was right.

B-students don't know everything about anything and are excellent at nothing. B-students do, however, know something about a lot of things, and they can complete almost any task with some modicum of competence. People often ask me: "As an entrepreneur, what exactly do you do?" My answer: "I do nothing. But I do it very well." Entrepreneurs are B-students. There is no one thing they do well. But there are many things they do well enough.

A-students, on the other hand, know a lot about one thing, whether it is technology or marketing or sales or finance. And they do this one thing extremely well. If they don't do it well, it bothers them. A-students want to do things perfectly all the time. This is a very bad trait for an entrepreneur, but a very good trait for a manager. More on this later.

The biggest downside of the entrepreneur's penchant to understand everything about nothing and a little bit about a lot of things is that they get bored quickly with any one task. The ability to focus and be patient is typically associated not with entrepreneurs but with managers. Entrepreneurs want results immediately, while managers are happy to wait, confident that if they execute perfectly over time the results will eventually follow.

An entrepreneur's short attention span allows him, or maybe even forces him, to think laterally. Because managers, on the other hand, can stay focused on one topic for a long period of time, they are able to—in fact prefer to—think in a more linear fashion. Lateral thinking is necessary in a start-up where the entrepreneur is constantly being pulled off course when plans don't go as planned, while linear thought is required in more mature companies where getting several hundred or several thousand people to stick to a plan is absolutely necessary to get anything done.

Whenever I speak to a group of business school students, I run them through a little game. I ask everyone who ever started a business to raise his or her hand. Typically, about half of the people do. I then ask those who are still running that same business to keep their hands up. Very few do. I then propose that those who raised their hands and then put them down are typical entrepreneurs: great at starting things, but maybe not so great at managing them. I conclude by recommending that these entrepreneurs take a look at the people who didn't raise their hands, jot down their names, give them a call next time they are about to start a business, and ask them to run it. Those people are the managers.

The most important thing to realize when you're a B-student entrepreneur is that you need A-student managers. You must listen to them. You have no choice. The good news is that

A-students must also listen to B-students, because B-students know about aspects of life and business that A-students know nothing about. While most A-students are really good at one thing, they tend to be completely out to lunch when it comes to most everything else. On the other hand, B-students are really good at being sort of good at everything. The sooner the B-students and the A-students understand and appreciate each other, the more productive everyone will be.

I had a standing bet with the programmers at Tripod, the aforementioned posse of hooligans, all of whom were A-students. The bet was that I could configure a web server before any of them could raise $1 million. The stakes of the bet: my founder's share of Tripod stock for their smaller share. To raise $1 million from investors, you must be able to talk intelligently, or at least convincingly, about every aspect of a business. To configure a web server—an extremely complicated task—you must forget about every other aspect of the business and focus on that alone. One of the reasons Tripod worked so well is that no programmer ever took me up on that bet. Neither side wanted to win. I knew just enough about how to configure a web server to scare them, and they were so good at configuring web servers that it scared me. We knew we needed each other.

There are, of course, exceptions to the A-student/B-student rule. We all know at least one. Take Bill Gates for instance, who both founded Microsoft and managed it into the largest corporation in the world. While Bill Gates never graduated from Harvard, he did go there and he did get A's. Or consider Warren Buffett, who started Berkshire Hathaway and manages it to this very day. Warren got his A's at Wharton. Or Matt Harris, my co-founder of Village Ventures, who not only helped start the company but also serves as its managing partner. I don't know Bill or Warren, but I do know Matt. And while I went to neither Harvard nor my local community college, I did go to college with Matt. And he got A's in half the time it took me to get B's. I know this is true because we shared a room, and I was in that room studying a hell of a lot more than he was.

In the end, the job of entrepreneurs is to attract, organize, and motivate A-student managers. And the only way we can do that is to realize, accept, and embrace the fact that we are B-students. One B and a slew of A's is a very good report card at any school.

4.

Great Is the Enemy of Good

There are thousands of business books, most of which contain not one useful word for entrepreneurs. But I'm sure they contain many useful concepts for managers. My friends who pride themselves on being good managers devour these books at the rate of several per week. God bless them. Remember, eventually these A-student managers have to show up and actually run the messes we B-student entrepreneurs create.

My sense is that the vast majority of business books use a lot of different words and stories to talk about the same topic: the transition that companies and their employees must make from "being good" to "being great." I don't know what the hell any of these books actually say (I'm opposed to reading most business press . . . more on this later), but they have titles like *Good to Great,* so I assume they help you elevate yourself from the drudgery of goodness to the shining light of greatness.

Greatness is exactly the wrong thing for entrepreneurs to strive for. I tell my colleagues: "Never let great be the enemy of good." A good decision made quickly is far better than a great decision made slowly.

There is no such thing as a great start-up, because every start-up can be improved upon. And most of the improvement happens between the first incarnation of a company and the tenth. Maybe by then, the company might well be considered great. And that is precisely the moment by which all of the true entrepreneurs will have left the building.

Start-ups are like extreme-skiing runs. The person who wins is the one who screws up the least and doesn't die. Success in a start-up is being around tomorrow, a lot of days in a row. The wisest thing my colleague Dick Sabot ever said to me was that "if we survive, we will succeed." Why? Because like the first run down an uncharted Alaskan peak, Tripod was such a big, crazy, and fundamentally innovative idea—allowing anyone in the world to publish whatever he or she wanted for free—that just surviving was going to look awfully good.

20

This type of logic confounds A-student managers. A's are great. B's are good. A's are success. B's are survival. A-students simply cannot allow their perfectionist minds to settle for good; they need great. But start-ups move too fast for greatness. Greatness, and the deliberate, perfectly-thought-through decision-making that greatness demands, is for companies like General Electric. This always has been, and always will be, true. Start-ups move more swiftly than established corporations. They don't have time to consider everything carefully or to perfect their products.

So if start-ups can't afford to be great, how do some succeed so wildly? My favorite illustration of this paradox is Project Mercury, the precursor to NASA that was commissioned to determine if humans could survive in outer space. Think of Project Mercury as the ultimate start-up, and think about NASA as the quintessential established company. The folks who worked on Project Mercury succeeded in actually figuring out that people could survive in outer space. Or, to be more accurate, they justified the creation of NASA and its very large budget. Without Project Mercury, the folks at NASA wouldn't be terribly busy today. Project Mercury was important, very successful, and certainly fundamentally innovative. But was it great?

Think about what NASA does today. People live in outer space for months at a time. Schoolteachers, businessmen, and celebrities are taking rides into orbit. We've got satellites circling most every planet, and we're researching ways to put whole cities in outer space. Now, these things are *great!* NASA is version ten of the product that Project Mercury entrepreneured. And it takes a whole lot of A-students, managing a large organization with an astronomical budget, to make NASA run smoothly and generate the consistent, steady, marginal improvements that greatness requires.

21

Maybe you've never heard of Project Mercury, but you've certainly heard of NASA. Maybe you've never heard of Tripod, but you've certainly heard of General Electric. Project Mercury and Tripod are good. NASA and General Electric are great. Start-ups are no place for greatness; leave that to the large, established companies. If your idea is big enough, and crazy enough, all you have to do is survive. If you survive, you will succeed.

5.

Start-Ups Attract Sociopaths

so·cio·path (noun): a person who is unwilling to behave in a way that is acceptable to society.

The first person I hired at Tripod was a complete sociopath. He avoided all social gatherings. He claimed to have played a key role in the actual creation of the Internet. He stole a framed picture from the desk of a colleague because he did not like the way he looked in it. He ultimately snookered me out of $60,000 of Tripod's capital (we only had $87,000 at the time), declared personal bankruptcy, and has managed since then, until this very day ten years later, to avoid even bumping into me in a town of six thousand people.

And I really like this guy.

Ordinary people don't agree to work for start-ups. They go get ordinary jobs. So, as an entrepreneur, you'd better like odd people, because that's who is going to agree to work with you. This is particularly true in the restaurant business. If you think computer programmers are lawless, long-haired, multi-pierced, tattooed hooligans, try hanging out with a crew of cooks for a night. At restaurants and technology companies, the drug-testing policy is: Bring your drugs in on Friday and we'll test them over the weekend.

In order to like odd people, you need not be odd yourself. I'm not. In fact, assuming you genuinely like odd people, the more ordinary you are, the more odd people will like you. It is an absolute sociological truth that odd people and ordinary people get a codependent kick out of being needed and liked by each other. But you can't fake it. If you're faking it, the odd people will know. They are smarter than you. Ordinary people get B's. Odd people get A's.

My all-time favorite odd person is Ethan Zuckerman, the leader of the first team of crazy programmers I hired and the individual most responsible for Tripod's success. When I first met Ethan, he was a radical leftist graduate student living in an upstate New York town of conservative farmers. Ethan was trying to complete what would have been the first master's in multimedia art ever awarded. I convinced him to come work at Tripod instead. Ethan is a six-foot-three, 275-pound black belt who always wears karate pants, hardly ever wears shoes, drinks two liters of Diet Pepsi a day, and is the drum master of a small tribe in central Ghana. A veritable God of Odd. Ethan was my utility player, my most trusted executive, and to this day is a very good friend.

After many long discussions, Ethan, Dick Sabot, and I decided that if Tripod was going to be a high-powered media company, it needed a high-powered editor. Enter Brian Hecht, one more in my great soaring circus of sociopaths.

Pat Sajak buys A's from Brian. He is a fascinating character: frighteningly smart, neurotic, mercurial, and sidesplittingly funny. Brian and I drank together all the time, went to parties together in New York City's Silicon Alley, and shared coaching duties for an elementary school soccer team in Williamstown. Brian was a trusted colleague, and we became good friends. Ethan, however, was skeptical, his finely tuned "oddar" having picked up trouble in the ranks.

Brian had been the editor of *The Harvard Crimson* and was, until he came to Tripod, working at ABC News in New York. Brian is a high-strung city kid. He talks a mile a minute, copyedits birthday cards he receives from friends, and has several life-threatening allergies. In the big city, he fit right in. But when someone with this particular cocktail of neuroses works fifteen-hour days in a small, traditional, isolated town in the mountains of northwestern Massachusetts, chaos is bound to ensue.

My most grueling test as an ordinary, odd-people-loving entrepreneur arrived with the clash of Brian and Ethan. It was a Tuesday at four in the morning, and I was asleep in my rarely visited bed. Nate Kurz was, on the other hand, wide-awake, programming at the office. While he worked at Tripod, Nate—number three on my all-time "Odd Guys I Love" list—lived out of a 1983 Aries K car, kept a "vacation" home in a depressed, old South Dakota farming town of two hundred people, and did not cash paychecks for years at a time. While making some routine updates, Nate tried to visit a story that he had posted a few months earlier on the main portion of the Tripod site, which was reserved for edited content rather than our members' unedited personal homepages. The story was an intimate account of how World War II had affected Nate's family. Brian, being the A-student editor that I was paying him to be, had removed Nate's story from the site.

I walked six miles with Nate that morning, from four until sunrise, talking him off the "Brian goes or I go" ledge. Nate and I ultimately agreed that everyone was wrong. He shouldn't have put the story on the site without Brian's approval, and Brian shouldn't have removed it without speaking to Nate—or at least to me—especially given the nature of the piece. Whatever. I could finally go to bed.

By the time I arrived at the office, at eleven, I could already sense I was about to enter a shit storm. Ethan, having enjoyed the luxury of a full five hours of sleep, had arrived at ten, just before Nate's bedtime. Ethan heard only Nate's side of the story, peppered, I'm sure, with a few unrelated "Brian is evil" rants. Ethan and I discussed the situation. Three hours later, we came to the same conclusion that Nate and I had come to seven hours before. Now it was two o'clock in the afternoon, *my* workday had not yet begun, and I knew that the Brian vs. Ethan clash was about to come to its inevitable head.

Sure enough, it did. For the next two months, Brian and Ethan were at each other's throats. They argued about every conceivable issue (and many inconceivable ones), and their arguments slowly halted all of Tripod's progress.

When the A-student odd people start to quarrel—I mean really fight—us ordinary B-student folk are in trouble. I needed both of these A-student sociopaths to make Tripod succeed; living without one of them was not an option. I had no choice but to pull out my most trusted odd-people-tricking trick. I was desperate. And I had built up enough trust with these guys that a little disingenuous dramatics wasn't going to discredit me. I called them both into my office, and after a good fifteen-minute soliloquy about how their infighting was crushing Tripod's unlimited potential to positively impact the lives of millions of people, I cried.

Ordinary people are repressed, and therefore cry less than odd people. So when ordinary people do in fact cry, odd people get really worried. And watching a six-foot-two, two-hundred-pound, blond-haired, blue-eyed, khaki-shorts-and-J.Crew-golf-shirt-wearing entrepreneur cry brought these guys to their knees. They never fought again.

If you're going to be an entrepreneur, be prepared to work with people who not only don't follow the rutted path of the masses but openly shun it. After all, that's why these people are willing to listen to you and your fundamentally innovative ideas in the first place. In working with odd people, you are in for some serious challenges. But you're also in for some serious treats. These are the smartest, most interesting people on the planet, and the fact that they are willing to give your ordinary B-getting ass the time of day should flatter you. And, occasionally, bring you to tears.

6.

Practice Blind Faith

I once read about a couple in Rutland, Vermont. They were ninety-seven years old, had been married for seventy-five years, and were filing for a divorce. They went to the town hall to obtain the necessary forms, and in an understandable fit of curiosity, the town clerk asked them: "After seventy-five years of marriage, why have you decided to divorce?"

The couple looked up innocently at the clerk and replied, "We stayed together for the kids, and now they're dead."

This is the type of devotion necessary to be an entrepreneur: devotion that makes little sense to rational human beings, devotion that is so crazy it's charming and inspires the support of others. When I got married, one of my groomsmen quipped that it was my second marriage. Tripod was my first.

The workload of a start-up is ridiculous. It's really not healthy. For eight years of my life, there were very few waking moments that Tripod did not completely consume. I rarely returned the phone calls of good friends. I routinely missed important family gatherings. I couldn't keep a steady girlfriend. To put it plainly, I didn't have enough time to maintain the sort of normal relationships typically associated with the human race.

A reporter once asked me, "What problem in your business

keeps you up at night?" I answered, "I'm not sleeping at night be-cause I'm sleeping at night." My biggest problem was time. In a good start-up, there are just not enough hours in the day to capi-talize on all the opportunities you see. Add to this the fact that I was a completely inexperienced kid, and the problem of time is exacerbated. I was like a bad driver late for a wedding with no di-rections to the ceremony. Every mile seemed like two.

What propels this limitless devotion of time and energy is the unconditional love that entrepreneurs must have for their start-ups. It can only be described as blind faith. It's astounding the number of people who will tell you that you and your idea are crazy. I have been thrown out of more than a thousand offices while building my six companies.

In 1994, I tried to convince the president of the largest mutual fund company in the world to make all of his offering documents available on the Internet. By his reaction, you would have thought that I was trying to convince him that all of his employees should ride unicorns to work. In 2000, I tried to convince America's largest investor in venture capital funds that there are great start-ups in Boise, Idaho. I would have done much better with the unicorn pitch. In 2001, a month before it was to be featured in *Gourmet* magazine as one of the top ten restaurants in Massachusetts, Mezze Bistro + Bar, Mezze's flagship restaurant, burned to the ground. And somehow, after several setbacks and many A-students telling me I was crazy, I kept going. I told you it pays to not be so smart.

Start-ups are fragile beings. Virtually every successful com-pany has, at one point in its life, come dangerously close to death. What revives these young start-ups is the work of passion-ate entrepreneurs with almost religious convictions about their company's products. Patient and supportive investors can also be a big help. Paul Maeder, the co-founder and managing partner of Highland Capital and the most entrepreneurial venture capitalist I know, once said to me, "Every successful investment I've ever made was at one point on life support." When a start-up goes south, and they all do at some point, entrepreneurs must work with their investors, colleagues, and customers to revive it.

Tripod, Village Ventures, and Mezze were all at one point at death's door. Independent of what other people may have thought of the business logic underlying those companies from the beginning, or the chances of their success when they stumbled, I was going to will them to succeed—because Tripod, Village Ventures, and Mezze are fundamentally innovative, morally compelling, and philosophically positive companies. I absolutely, completely, one hundred percent believe that the world is a better place with these companies than it is without them. And I knew that there were lots of people out there who would agree with me. I just had to find them.

I practiced my blind faith hard, and in the end, I found the believers. But even the believers started out as skeptics. And looking back on it now, I get the sense that many of the believers were a lot like the town clerk of Rutland, Vermont: unsure of the underlying logic of what they were about to get involved in, but inspired by the raw energy and sheer audacity of it all.

7.

Learn to Love the Word "No"

With only seven months to get Tripod into the black before our venture capital ran out, I hired a vice president of sales to help me bring in the much-needed revenue. He had been in the traditional advertising-sales business for several years, which seemed to make him the perfect hire. However, selling advertising on the Internet in 1996 was like selling meat to vegans. People said "no" to this guy a lot. When I asked him about this, he gave me a very astute answer: "Bo, products are not bought, they are sold. The sales process begins when the customer says 'No.' "

Entrepreneurs hear the word "no" more than anyone else in business. And for good reason: Entrepreneurs are pursuing fundamentally innovative projects, and the vast majority of typical business people are lemmings. Why the hell would they support, with their time or their money, someone doing something new? Instead, they say "No."

Most business people are not paid to take risks. No one ever lost his or her job for buying a piece of software from Microsoft, or placing an advertisement in *People* magazine. But people do lose their jobs when they do something new or different, like buying a product from or making an investment in a start-up. So when you ask someone at General Electric to believe that you can control the clouds, don't expect her to get all excited; it's much easier for her to simply say, "No."

So entrepreneurs must learn to love the word "no." It's a perverse but necessary tool for survival.

The first time I realized I loved the word "no" was when I applied to college. I was determined to attend Williams College, one of the world's most selective institutions of higher learning. One of every five people who apply to Williams gets in, which is one of every hundred who seriously think about applying and one of every thousand who ask their high school guidance counselor if they should apply. I didn't have a prayer of getting accepted. I was, after all, a B-student.

And sure enough, I got the thin envelope: the one with no information about when school starts, or what dorm you're in, or who your roommate will be. Instead, it just contains that nicely worded letter, the one that when you cut through all the flowery language simply says "no."

I needed a plan. The customer had said "no," and the sales process was just beginning. Figuring that the admissions committee of this elite school had probably seen and heard just about everything, I decided to take a bold, direct, and unorthodox approach. I got the telephone number of the assistant director of admissions, a man named Cornelius (Corny) Raiford. I called Corny up and told him:

"Hi, my name is Bo Peabody, and I reject your rejection."

There was a long silence. "Excuse me?" he said.

"I want to go to Williams College," I continued. "And with all due respect, I think the admissions committee has made a mistake. And I'd like to work with you to correct it. I am formally rejecting your rejection. I'm coming to Williams. Not next year perhaps, but at some point. I'm in no rush. I have all the time in

31

the world, and I plan to send an application in to Williams every year until I'm accepted."

There was another long silence. At this point, I figure Corny is either going to play ball with me or transfer my call to the police. Corny cleared his throat, and said, "I appreciate your desire to attend Williams. I'm not sure I've ever received a call like this, so let's see what we can do." For the next few months, I worked with Corny to build a yearlong program during which I'd remedy several of the deficiencies (read: B's) he saw in my application. That next year, I re-applied to Williams, and was granted early admission to the class of 1994.

Most people would simply accept the rejection. Don't. Ever. Train yourself not to shut down when you hear the word "no." **32** That is in fact just the time to really start fighting. No human being likes to say "no" to another human being. When he does, he is at his weakest moment. Take that opportunity, and start selling.

8.

Prepare to Be Powerless

When you're an entrepreneur, even getting a "no" is a triumph. It's a sign that your customer is at least marginally engaged with you and your proposal. The much more maddening situation is when your calls are not returned, your e-mails ignored, and the FedEx describing your fundamentally innovative concept is collecting dust on the desk of some underworked, overpaid, gutless, balding, fifty-five-year-old Vice President of Worrying at some Fortune 500 company. I'll take a "no" any day. At least then I know I've got one of his ears out of his ass and on the telephone.

Forgive me. While the above thought (and perhaps even more violent versions) may go through your head at your desk while you enjoy your fifth box of macaroni and cheese that week, it must never enter your head while working. The fact is: These vice presidents are busy people, running very important functions at profitable, successful companies. And you absolutely need them. These guys are the A-students. You, your B's, and your fundamentally innovative concept are not even close to being on their radar screens. You are, in short, powerless.

Ultimately, however, if you send enough e-mail, log enough voice mail, and spend enough money on FedEx, these guys *will* return your call. As it turns out, they are human beings, too. But when they do return your call, they will not apologize for their tardiness, they will not acknowledge the numerous voice mails and e-mails that they deleted, and they will definitely not have opened any of the five FedEx envelopes you sent them. And— even worse than all that—they will talk to you in a monotone, as if this is the most annoying thing they will have to do that day. Which it probably is.

But this is your chance, your one chance. You've got him on the phone. Even the most disinterested bastard will listen to you for sixty seconds. And remember, guys like this have a fiduciary responsibility to their shareholders to continue the conversation if they hear even one thing during those sixty seconds that may help them raise profits at their company. So with an enthusiastic voice that acknowledges none of the injustices inflicted on you by this pencil-pushing slug, launch into your elevator pitch: sixty seconds about how you can help this gutless guy do his boring job better.

If you've done your research, tailored the content of your pitch, used the right tone, and hit on a little luck, you will spend the next fifteen minutes discussing how your company can help his company. This is the most valuable fifteen minutes an entrepreneur can have. Listen carefully and take copious notes. Believe it or not, you and your fundamentally innovative concept have just been given the opportunity of a lifetime.

Perhaps even worse than that first fifteen-minute phone call is the panic-inducing process of closing your first sale. Entrepreneurs are always the underdogs, trying to sell their products to people who don't think they need them (or at least don't yet know they need them). Entrepreneurs are therefore always low on the to-do list of the people they are trying to do business with. Ironically, though, these people are always number one on the entrepreneur's to-do list. "Sell product to Microsoft" makes sense as a first item on a to-do list. "Buy product from Tripod" just doesn't have the same ring.

The result of this mismatch in priorities is that the entrepreneur is often left in limbo, wondering what happened to the customer he or she had been successfully courting. It's shocking the number of times I've been in the middle of negotiating a deal with a prospective customer when he has simply disappeared for a week or longer. Twenty days of twice-daily back-and-forth phone calls, and then one day he's gone, with no explanation. Is this polite? No. Good business etiquette? Not even close. But it happens all the time.

In this situation, it's very easy, and perfectly reasonable, to indulge your sense of powerlessness, panic, and assume that your big fish has spit out the hook. But that's almost never true. In the vast majority of cases, your prospective customer will eventually reconnect and produce a decent excuse for his silence. Sure, the excuses are often strange, and indicate dysfunction on the part of your customer's employer. But that's the way it goes.

During these moments of silence, good entrepreneurs don't panic. The fact is that you can never know what is going on in someone else's business, or in his life. What you can count on as an entrepreneur is that for a prospective customer, most of those things will come before he talks to you.

The situation is compounded if you are young. And because technology is one of the major drivers of entrepreneurial activity, and young people are the major drivers of technology, young entrepreneurs are more prevalent now than twenty years ago. I started Tripod when I was nineteen years old. It was very difficult to get anyone to take me seriously. And except for the brief moment in time when young Internet entrepreneurs were in vogue, I went to great lengths to hide my age. I had no choice. The prejudice against age is rampant in the business world. Even now, when I'm thirty-three, people look at me funny, wondering whether or not I've paid my dues long enough to deserve their attention.

Young or old, entrepreneurs have to accept that creating fundamentally innovative products and trying to sell them to executives at established companies is an uphill battle. The executives have power and you don't. Get used to it.

9.

The Best Defense Is a Gracious Offense

I was in a bar one night with my friend Anthony, who happens to be of Italian heritage. A jovial fellow sitting next to us asked Anthony, "Will you be offended if I tell you a good Italian joke?"

Anthony answered, "No, I won't be offended, but I get to tell you one first."

A little taken aback, the guy responded, "Okay, sure."

"What's black and blue and floats down rivers?" Anthony asked, the bartender and everyone sitting at the bar now listening in.

"I don't know," the guy replied.

"Guys who tell Italian jokes."

Everyone laughed, and the would-be comedian, who now found himself the butt of a good joke, bought us a round of drinks.

Obviously, it's not polite to tell ethnic jokes. And Anthony was certainly within his rights to be defensive, which would have made the whole situation awkward. Instead, Anthony devised a gracious offense, and turned the situation into an opportunity to both make his point and make a friend. And, not insignificantly, to get us both a free drink.

No matter what, above all else, remember that in business it never pays to get indignant in any way. In every meeting, in every situation, you must always, always, always be gracious. The business world is a small place; what goes around comes around. Your ability to remain gracious will be tested often, and you will constantly be tempted to become defensive.

In 1993, I had breakfast with Steve Case, the founder of America Online, which at the time was one of only a handful of online services. Steve is also a Williams College alumnus, and it was on that basis that he agreed to have breakfast with me, which was pretty gracious of him in the first place.

Over omelets and orange juice, which he graciously paid for, Steve graciously told me that Tripod would never work. He explained that AOL, CompuServe, and Prodigy had the online services game locked up and that there was no room for newcomers, much less a kid, his economics professor, and a handful of crazy computer programmers. I argued, graciously, that the market for online services would be huge and that there would be room for companies like Tripod, which had a more focused approach, segmenting the market both demographically and psycho-graphically. Steve graciously disagreed. It was an extremely gracious breakfast during which nothing got done.

Five years later, Steve graciously offered to buy Tripod for 60 million gracious dollars.

We did not end up accepting that offer from AOL, and instead sold Tripod to Lycos for reasons unrelated to our breakfast or the way I felt about Steve or AOL. But it was a good example of why always being gracious, and never being indignant, is critical for entrepreneurs. When you leave a meeting or telephone conversation, no matter the outcome, the other person should *always,* at the very least, like you.

Perhaps the best example of graciousness I have encountered took place when I was on the receiving end. After a restaurant has had a fire, and certainly after it has had a "total loss" fire like Mezze Bistro + Bar did, the catastrophe itself is further compounded by what happens next: negotiating with your insurance company to cover the damages.

There isn't much positive to say about the insurance business. No one likes it, not the people who buy insurance policies or the people who sell them. It just is what it is: an unfortunate but necessary part of life. Negotiating with insurance companies is perhaps the most entrepreneurial of tasks. You always have fewer resources, less time, less experience, and less power than the insurance company. Yet, even as they condescend to you and challenge every ounce of personal integrity you possess, you have to sell them your product and be gracious the entire time.

About two weeks after our fire, as we were preparing the supporting documentation for our insurance claim, the owners of Main Street Café, our biggest competitor, called and offered us access to their sales figures. They wanted to help us build a better case. It was an incredibly gracious gesture. We took them up on their offer and strengthened our claim as a result.

Nine months later, while we were *still* negotiating with the insurance company, I received a call from one of the owners of Main Street Café, the same man who had offered us the sales figures. He explained that for a variety of reasons they were selling the business. Knowing that we were in the market for a new space, he wondered if we'd be interested in purchasing it. Their asking price, while fair, was probably a little higher than we needed to pay, given their situation. But I didn't negotiate. Two months later, we had a deal to buy Main Street Café, and after some quick renovations, Mezze Bistro + Bar was re-opened.

We did finally settle our claim with the insurance company. I am confident that, thanks to the information we received from Main Street Café, we came out better than even on the whole deal. Being gracious and recognizing graciousness always pays dividends. You won't always be successful in maintaining your cool. I'm certainly not. But the more often you stay calm and gracious, the better off you and your business will be.

10.

Don't Believe Your Own Press. In Fact, Don't Read.

Marty Liebowitz, the vice chairman and chief investment officer of TIAA-CREF, one of the largest pension funds in the world, once said to me, "Thank God they created the word 'muffin' or I'd be eating a cupcake for breakfast." Words are incredibly powerful and influence our behavior, sometimes causing us to do things that we would never normally do.

It is for just this reason that I harbor a tremendous amount of guilt about my place in entrepreneurial culture. I fear that perhaps thousands of well-intentioned people wasted hundreds of thousands of hours pursuing entrepreneurial projects in part because of what they read in the press about me. I created a sort of playboy persona for myself as the CEO of Tripod. Pictures of me skiing, mountain-biking, drinking beer, skateboarding in the office, and attending meetings in shorts, Birkenstocks, and a baseball cap graced several major media outlets. From *Forbes* to ABC's *Nightline,* from *BusinessWeek* to *People,* from MTV to *Spin,* the media broadcast images of me doing just about everything but working.

I absolutely, completely, one hundred percent sold myself to the media to promote Tripod. Together, we created this image of the "Slacker CEO": an athletic, shaggy-haired, perpetually mellow twenty-four-year-old making millions of dollars while barely lifting a finger.

This image was broadcast not just in the United States but also to most of Europe. In five days during the summer of 1999, I jetted from Madrid to Milan, to Hamburg, to Paris, and finally to London, attending launch parties for Tripod Europe, staying in first-class hotels, and internationalizing the Slacker CEO myth of which I had become the archetypal example.

Hell, who wouldn't want to be an entrepreneur? I was a rock star. And I was the only person who knew it wasn't true. Friends would ask me, "What's it like to be a famous international Internet CEO?" "I'm not a famous international Internet CEO," I would answer. "But I play one on TV."

Working with the media was the most important job I had at Tripod. Period. Twenty-four-year-old Bo Peabody, with his hip Internet company in the mountains, was a perfectly packaged pied piper for the story of the decade. I was not only Tripod's poster child, I was shilling the whole goddamn Internet. And when it came to promoting these two things, the only self-respecting thing I ever did was turn down an interview on *Montel*. How noble.

I've often joked to people that 90 percent of Tripod's value was in the amount of press we received in such a concentrated period of time. Sitting at a board meeting, lamenting our anemic revenue, I once joked to the board of directors that rather than actually running ads on the Tripod site, I'd sell potential advertising customers the opportunity that I might mention them in an article or wear their logo on my baseball cap. The board didn't laugh. They asked me to look into whether or not this plan was possible.

A lot was left out of all those articles. The one-hundred-hour workweeks. The anxiety attacks. The crashed cars and missed planes. The times I had to tell colleagues that we couldn't make payroll. The years of a $12,000 salary. Night after night after night of pasta dinners and stress-relieving Advil "cocktails." The countless meetings with absolute assholes who had no interest in learning about the Internet, the single most significant business innovation of their lifetimes. Pleading to venture capitalists for financing. Firing perfectly pleasant people when they didn't perform. In the late nineties, this reality did not sell newspapers and magazines. Baseball caps and Birkenstocks did.

Had I actually begun to believe what was being said about me in the press, I would never have sold Tripod when I did. I would have reasoned, instead, that I was in fact a genius, and that I should take complete credit for the great things happening to my company. Never mind that Tripod had little revenue, no profits, and an unproven business model; we should take this horse public! "Yeah," I could have said, "I am smart, not lucky, and I can defy economic gravity. I am in control!" Wrong. Tripod was all hat and no cattle. Had we taken it public, we would most likely have failed, and everyone, including many unsuspecting individual investors, would have lost a lot of money.

43

I was not, however, completely immune to the media frenzy. Following the sale of Tripod to Lycos, what personal money I did not invest in bonds or real estate I invested in more than twenty different Internet start-ups. Only five of these companies are still in business. The others are gone, along with a few million of my dollars.

The quickest way to completely tank your company is to wholeheartedly believe what you read in the press, especially if it happens to be about you. The vast majority of the press is not interested in covering what is actually happening. They are interested in covering what they think people want to think is actually happening. Everything is sensationalized. In 1999, it was sensationalized on the positive side, and in 2002, it was sensationalized on the negative side. It's never exactly accurate. As it turns out, accuracy can be quite boring. And quite boring does not sell newspapers and magazines.

Yet I'm amazed at how much most entrepreneurs read: a stack of business magazines in their briefcases; My Yahoo! on constant refresh in their web browsers; CNBC on a television in their offices. When do these people ever get the opportunity to think about *their* business? To think creatively about *their* strategies and *their* products? Ask yourself: As an entrepreneur, what are you gaining from reading about other people's companies, especially when it's so often sensationalized, and therefore not entirely accurate? I'll tell you what you're getting: unfocused, unrealistic, and scared.

I watched one of the better entrepreneurs I've ever known ruin his company by falling prey to what I call the "Last Article Syndrome." He read and read and read and read. And every time he read about something new, he went back to his company and implemented it. He was afraid he'd miss "the next big thing," and that he'd wake up one morning and see it on his competitor's website instead of on his own.

Remember VRML? Of course you don't. It was silly. VRML, or Virtual Reality Mark-up Language, was a late nineties technological phenomenon that turned a perfectly functional website into a three-dimensional mess, visible only to the ten people in the world who had cable modems surgically attached to their spinal cords. This otherwise very smart entrepreneur took his very successful site and reprogrammed the whole thing in very stupid

VRML. He became unfocused and scared, and forgot that most of his customers were still dialing in to the Internet over tiny little copper wires called telephone lines. Had this entrepreneur simply stayed focused on *his* products and on *his* customers, rather than becoming distracted by what everyone else was doing (or not doing, as the case may be), he could have built a very successful company. Instead, he went bankrupt in 1998, when going bankrupt was a difficult thing to do.

Without question, the worst and most dangerous example of this "constantly reading" phenomenon is the BlackBerry. These little handheld devices send your e-mail to you anywhere in the world, so that you can fill all your free time reading penis-enlargement spam and responding to the generally non-time-sensitive queries of your colleagues. I know people who leave the dinner table to go to the bathroom to check e-mail. This is insane. Of course, it's better than the assholes who sit at the dinner table and answer their e-mail. The best use you can make of a Black-Berry is to buy them for all of your competitors. They'll never have time for another creative thought.

Managing your information intake is one of the most important tasks for an entrepreneur. You should err on the side of less. Daily, you should read only *The Wall Street Journal*. Then read *The New York Times* on Sunday and choose one of the several reputable weekly or monthly business magazines. That is all you need. If you're doing something fundamentally innovative, then there shouldn't be much in the news for you anyway. By definition, the news has already happened. And the more you fill your head with the past, the less room there is to think about the future.

11.

Always Be Selling Your Stock

Entrepreneurs have one job: to create a market for the stock in their start-up. Anyone who tells you otherwise is wrong. Anyone who tells you to spend your days managing product development, tweaking the budget, or reviewing the sales and marketing effort is wrong. Certainly, these are all important jobs. But these jobs should be the primary responsibility of the A-students you've hired. For the entrepreneur, these jobs are secondary to The Job: to create a market for your start-up's stock.

Many start-ups are not profitable in their early years of operation. To cover the losses accrued along the path to profitability, entrepreneurs must raise capital. Unlike public companies, for whom there is a well-defined architecture for accessing capital, start-ups are forced to piece together financing through a Byzantine and often inhospitable system of private investors.

The people in this system who are most likely to buy your stock are called venture capitalists. Entrepreneurs and venture capitalists end up spending a great deal of time with each other. Having been on both sides of the table, I can tell you that the biggest irony of modern capitalism is that innovation relies on the productive working relationship between these two groups of people. Entrepreneurs and venture capitalists often have very different personalities and very different approaches to their lives and careers.

Venture capitalists, or "VCs" as they are commonly known, operate with a bit of a herd mentality, and prefer to see their fellow VCs interested in a company before they signal any interest themselves. Compared to entrepreneurship, there's nothing truly adventurous about venture capital. Venture capitalists are simply capitalists. They want to make money. And the best way to make money is to manage money: to take someone else's cash, invest it in a diversified fashion such that it turns into more cash, and then take a cut of the profits.

Entrepreneurs, on the other hand, are not diversified. They put all of their proverbial eggs in one basket. If an entrepreneur decides to put ten years of his life into one company, and that company fails, he loses. If it succeeds, he wins, and wins big, far bigger than the VC. But for every successful VC, there are nine unsuccessful entrepreneurs. Now, that's adventure. But it's also not particularly clever betting. Entrepreneurs are B-students. Venture capitalists are A-students.

There are, of course, exceptions. Some VCs were once entrepreneurs, and remain so at heart. And many go through the very entrepreneurial process of starting their own venture capital fund from scratch. However, these entrepreneurial VCs quickly realize the acute need to bring in the pure A-student VCs to help them manage the fund. The best venture capital firms have a healthy mix of entrepreneurs and managers. This allows them to make sound investment decisions but also understand entrepreneurs and be helpful to them during the more fluid process of actually executing a business plan.

To successfully create a market for their stock, entrepreneurs must realize that venture capitalists are insanely busy people.

Most venture capital firms receive thousands of business plans every year. And out of every one thousand business plans they receive, one hundred might get fully reviewed. And of those one hundred that get fully reviewed, one might actually end up getting funded. Friends, family members, investment bankers, fellow VCs, entrepreneurs they meet at conferences, and even random people they sit next to on airplanes are sending their business plans to VCs with reckless abandon. This all makes it very difficult for VCs to separate the good business plans from the bad ones.

But VCs are competitive people. As such, they respond well to auction environments. When I first raised money for Tripod, I was a complete nobody. I was twenty-three and looked like a sixteen-year-old. I had no business experience (other than my lawn-mowing/snowblowing/sealcoating empire) and was trying to start a company that offered consumers a service through the Internet, a communication medium that most people, including a majority of the VCs I met, had never used. I quickly realized that the only way to get a venture capitalist interested in Tripod was to get that venture capitalist interested in the fact that other venture capitalists were interested in Tripod, thereby creating an auction.

The relative ease of creating an auction for your stock is dependent on two things: (1) timing and (2) the presentation of your business plan.

Timing is out of your control. Period. In 1999, some of the worst entrepreneurs and business plans created frothy auctions for their stock. In 2002, some of the best entrepreneurs and business plans went completely unfunded.

The piece you can control is how you present your business plan. It is an art. And to do it well, you must learn how to sell. Selling a start-up business plan requires you to predict the future. If your start-up is growing quickly, then a snapshot of what is happening on any given day does not tell the whole story. You must peer carefully into the future and give your investors a window into what will be, rather than just what is. And then you have to work like hell to make sure the future you predicted actually happens.

The fact is that no one, including you, has any idea how big and interesting your company might ultimately become. Start-ups are simply educated guesses riddled with assumptions. In some cases, those assumptions are backed up by some research: In 2004, there were 1.5 million people with cellular phones in Paraguay. But in most cases, these assumptions are WAGs (wild-ass guesses): In 2005, 10 percent of Paraguayans with cellular phones will subscribe to my new wireless messaging service.

The best and the worst thing about a start-up is that there is very little data to assess, very few facts to ponder. It's your words and ideas against everyone else's. So you have to sell. And the best VCs know this. Of course, VCs are assessing your company, but they are much more interested in assessing you and your ability to think clearly, quickly, and creatively as you sell them stock in your big, ambitious Alaskan peak of an idea. They do this because they know that once you leave their offices, with *their* money in *your* bank account, your most important job is selling a bigger, bolder, and higher-priced version of your stock to the next group of investors.

When I first pitched Tripod to NEA, the VCs there came back and told me: "We think your revenue assumptions are too modest. Our financial model suggests that this can be a bigger business."

"Great," I responded. "Then my forecasts are conservative, and we'll all be pleasantly surprised when I exceed them."

49

"No, you don't get it," they replied. "We want you to change your forecasts to be more aggressive, and then we want you to try to hit those numbers. We understand you might fall short, but that's okay."

"Ah, er, um . . . yeah, sure, whatever . . . I'll change my forecasts."

What NEA wanted me to do was think big. Good VCs know that the key ingredient in a start-up's growth is not how big the company actually *will* be but how big the entrepreneur thinks it *can* be. And good VCs also know that salesmanship is an important skill for an entrepreneur to have. It is the force that propels a start-up forward and challenges the entrepreneur to achieve more than he might otherwise as he constantly tries to fulfill the future he's predicted.

Talking with venture capitalists is just one of the many times entrepreneurs will need to know how to sell. But many entrepreneurs will never need to sell their stock to VCs in order to raise capital. Some of the best entrepreneurs I know have never talked to a VC. Their businesses—a restaurant, a record store, or a reseller of computer equipment—have hard assets and/or generate cash flow from their customers quickly enough that they can raise capital through loans from family or traditional banks, or even fund their own expansion through profits.

But don't fool yourself: The process of getting a loan from a bank still requires selling, as does generating cash flow from customers. I know a restaurateur who met with thirty banks before one finally agreed to loan him $10,000. Once that bank agreed to do it, all the other banks wanted a piece of the action. Sound familiar? An entrepreneur is always selling. But most important, an entrepreneur must always be selling his stock.

12.

Know What You Don't Know

As important as it is to know how to sell your way through important business situations, it is equally important to be able to recognize when there is in fact a right answer to a difficult question and you have no idea what it is.

The final step in the process of raising venture capital is pitching your idea to the entire partnership of the venture capital firm that you are courting. For me and Dick, that meant a two-hour meeting at the Baltimore headquarters of NEA. Ten of their partners sat around the largest mahogany conference table that I've ever seen, and three or four more partners from NEA's West Coast office attended via videoconference. For a fresh-faced twenty-four-year-old still clutching his college diploma, it was absolutely terrifying.

The meeting started well. I was on my game, giving a solid pitch about how Tripod was well positioned to dominate the new Internet online services business. The NEA partners seemed quite convinced. Dick and I had researched our facts, practiced our presentation for a week, and had good answers to all of their questions. But about ninety minutes into the meeting, one of the senior NEA partners asked a question we hadn't anticipated (good VCs have a way of doing this). I don't even remember what the question was, but it was tough. And he knew he'd rocked us back on our heels.

I looked over at Dick, looked down at my notes, looked around the room at the other NEA partners, glanced at the funky pixilated images of the NEA partners on the West Coast, and proceeded to do what I always did in such situations: I started selling. I wasn't two sentences into my pitch when Dick calmly reached over and put his hand on my arm. It was one of those fatherly gestures that told me, "Hold on, son." The room went silent, and the senior partner who'd stumped us leaned back in his chair, satisfied that he had us in a corner.

Then, in his professorial tone that implied omniscience, Dick said, "We don't know." Not a word came from around the mahogany conference table. The senior NEA partner eyeballed the two of us from across the table and finally broke the silence. "You're right," he said in a tone that conveyed his own fatherly instincts. "You don't know. That is the right answer." And at that moment, it all fell into place. Within sixty minutes of that exchange, NEA produced a proposal outlining the terms of their offer. We then consulted with our advisers. Sixty minutes after that, we agreed to sell 33 percent of Tripod to NEA for $3 million.

A few years later, Peter Barris, NEA's managing partner and one of the best venture capitalists I've ever worked with, told me, "Bo, I like you because you ask questions. And you don't have cement ears." Peter was referring to the hundreds of times I had simply told him that I didn't know the answer to a question and that I needed his help to figure it out. But I'm sure Peter also had in mind that moment in NEA's offices when, in a pressure-packed situation, I displayed to him and his partners that I know what I don't know. Rather than arguing that I had the answer to Peter's partner's question, I just let Dick's "We don't know" answer sit.

52

Knowing what you don't know is vital in the restaurant business, where people with radically divergent skill sets must cooperate in a real-time environment to produce a product whose quality can go from perfect to packaged in a matter of seconds. Restaurants are roughly made up of three units: the front of the house (wait staff, bus staff, and bartenders), the back of the house (chefs, cooks, and dishwashers), and the general manager.

The front of the house is like a theater. For eight hours a night, actors stage a show for which they have no script. The audience, rather than just watching passively, is participating actively, interacting with the actors and, in many cases, providing the majority of the entertainment. When that night's show is over, the audience leaves and goes out into the world as either your best marketers or agents of business sabotage. If a member of the audience liked the show, he will tell two friends. And if he didn't like it, he will tell ten.

The back of the house is best described as a fine-art assembly line. The same perfect painting must be produced hundreds of times per night. Meat, fish, and vegetables are the canvases onto which carefully mixed sauces are painted. One poorly prepared canvas, one hastily mixed paint, or one botched brushstroke, and a finished product can go quickly from fine art to finger painting.

Finally, there is the general manager, who acts as a one-person marketing and accounting staff. Greeting all customers graciously, treating preferred customers like royalty, diffusing difficult situations in both the front and the back of the house, and making sure that the numbers all add up at the end of the night, the general manager is the eyes, ears, and nose of a restaurant.

When you put actors, painters, marketers, and accountants in the same room, you'd better hope that they know what they don't know. If the actors think they can paint, you are screwed. And if the accountants think they can act *or* paint, you are really screwed. But if everyone knows what she knows, and knows what she doesn't know, the show will get rave reviews.

In business, admitting that you don't know something is difficult. First, you have to admit it to yourself. And then, in order for it to make any difference, you have to admit it to your colleagues. You can't take the second step until you successfully complete the first. Unfortunately, most people can't even find the first step, much less take it.

Conclusion

A good friend of mine once ran the Seattle Marathon in a very respectable three hours and twenty minutes. While standing in the finish area, he found himself chatting with the winner, who had run the race in two hours and fifty minutes.

A woman approached the two of them. "I want to congratulate you," she said to the winner. "And tell you how much I admire you. I just finished in my best time of five hours and ten minutes, and here you are running the race in under three hours. You are amazing."

The winner paused and thought for a moment about what the nice woman had told him. "Actually, ma'am," he replied, "you are the amazing one. I can't imagine running for five hours."

The world is full of different perspectives. And nowhere is this more true than in the world of entrepreneurship. It is impossible for anyone to completely understand the myriad variables affecting someone else's start-up. Hell, you can't even understand the variables that affect your *own* business. From the vast variety of start-up business concepts being pursued to the endlessly intricate personal relationships between co-founders, every entrepreneurial situation is truly unique.

This book may or may not be useful to you and whatever entrepreneurial situation you are in or might be thinking of joining. I don't profess to have written anything that is inarguably true, or universally applicable. There is, however, one overarching theme that ties all of my observations together. One thing that I am absolutely, completely, one hundred percent sure you should take heed of, and never forget: understanding the difference between being lucky and being smart.

The power to understand this crucial difference comes from one simple source: the ability to always keep your ego in check. Your ego is both the most dangerous and the most useful weapon in your entrepreneurial arsenal. When used wisely, ego helps entrepreneurs craft their start-ups' missions, work hard, and keep blind faith in their companies, even in the face of heavy scrutiny. Ego also gives entrepreneurs the confidence to sell their start-ups to partners, customers, and investors, and the courage to act like famous international CEOs even when they know they are really just playing a role. And ego is the force that allows entrepreneurs to get comfortable with their powerlessness and learn to love the word "no" instead of panicking in the face of it.

On the other hand, when allowed to run amok, ego keeps entrepreneurs from knowing what they don't know and tempts them to believe their own press. Ego is also the culprit when entrepreneurs, unhappy with their B's, try to achieve greatness and cling to their role as founder rather than turning their companies over to more capable managers. And ego is to blame when entrepreneurs can't work with odd people who are clearly smarter than they are, or when they fail to remain calm and gracious in all business situations.

Use your ego when it is called for, and check it at the door when you sense that it will get in the way. Unchecked egos are the most destructive force in start-ups, and in business in general.

I have often dreamed of a study that somehow measures the impact of ego on workplace productivity. The results, I imagine, would be staggering, with as much as a 50 percent increase in productivity resulting from the eradication of egos. In an ego-free company, all good ideas from all sources would be implemented. Managers would hire only people smarter than they, and would never spend valuable time worrying about who gets credit for what. Meetings would be shorter, as no one would feel the need to drone on about nonsense in an effort to impress his colleagues and managers. In a business world devoid of egos, profits would rise, salaries would increase, and unemployment would plummet. In all seriousness: A number of the planet's problems would be solved.

But it will never happen. As it turns out, businesses consist of human beings, and most human beings have either tragically fragile egos or uncontrollably big ones. All we can do is make an effort to control our own egos. As hard as it may be, there are real incentives to do so.

If I had let my ego go unchecked, I would never have let those crazy programmers put the Homepage Builder on Tripod. The Homepage Builder, after all, was not my idea. Moreover, it *was* the idea of people who were clearly smarter than I was. Someone who was insecure would have declared the Homepage Builder a distraction, a waste of time, inappropriate for the Tripod audience, too expensive, too risky, or any of the other excuses that those with fragile egos use to fortify their own power bases.

But the fact is, the Homepage Builder was the foundation of Tripod's success. The day we launched that little piece of software, we enrolled more members than in the entire previous month. It was like watching the Gold Rush all over again: The automated-membership counter ticked away as hundreds of strangers from all over the world signed up on Tripod and staked a claim to their little piece of Internet real estate.

In the end, my original idea for Tripod—practical advice for college students—was completely consumed by the popularity of the Tripod Homepage Builder. At one point, Tripod was the eighth most trafficked site on the Internet. Our membership base spanned every age and more than forty countries. Now, as part of the Terra Lycos network, Tripod has 40 million members, from virtually every country on the planet. Had I stuck religiously to my original idea, the best thing that could have happened to Tripod would have been my being fired as its CEO. But more likely, it would have ended up on the pile of failed dot-com start-ups that now symbolize an age of ego and excess.

Without the Homepage Builder, Tripod most likely would have failed, and my life would have taken a different direction. Without the success of Tripod under my belt, Village Ventures would probably not have received the funding and support it has. And without Village Ventures, the four other start-ups I helped found—Mezze, VoodooVox, Waterfront Media, and FilmFree Entertainment—would most likely not be flourishing to the degree that they are. Was I lucky? You bet your ass I was lucky. But I was also smart: smart enough to realize that I was getting lucky.

58

ACKNOWLEDGMENTS

Thanks:

For encouraging me to write: Caroline

For love and support: Mom and Dad, Mark, Caroline, and my
entire extended family

For great partnerships: Peter Barris, Bob Davis, Gil Fuchsberg,
Scott Hamilton, Matt Harris, Habib Kairouz, Mike Keriakos,
Warren Lammert, Paul Maeder, Samantha McCuen, Anson
Montgomery, Mark Nunnelly, Chris Pasko, Marty Peretz, Ted
Philip, Eyal Rimmon, Nancy Thomas, Peter Willmott, and
Ben Wolin

For teaching me what a great partnership is: Dick Sabot

For wisdom and hard work: Michael Barach, Joann Bates,
Paul Debraccio, Joshua Field, Matt Goldberg, Brian Hecht,
Ben Jones, Bob Kraus, Bruce Ludemann, Sean Marsh, Jane
Martin, Steve Massicotte, Kevin McCormack, Gina Raimondo,
Peter Rankin, Margaret Gould Stewart, Scott Walker,
Matt Warta, Kara Weber, Don Zereski, and Ethan Zuckerman

For fond memories: Frank Marz

For following dreams and doing the right thing: Brett Hershey

APPENDIX

Companies co-founded by Bo Peabody:

Tripod, Inc.

Co-founded by Brett Hershey, Bo Peabody, and Dick Sabot in 1992, Tripod is currently owned by Terra Lycos, a wholly owned subsidiary of Daum Communications Corporation, a leading South Korean technology firm that recently bought Terra Lycos from Telefonica, a Spanish telecommunications conglomerate. Tripod has been translated into fifteen languages and, with millions of members worldwide, is one of the leading personal publishing sites on the Internet.

Waterfront Media, Inc.

Formed by the merger of Streetmail (co-founded by Matt Harris, Anson Montgomery, and Bo Peabody in 1998) and Agora Media (co-founded by Benjamin Wolin and Michael Keriakos in 2002), Waterfront works with experts in fields such as fitness, dieting, dating, religion, and personal finance to produce and market their messages online through subscription-based products such as southbeachdiet.com and deniseaustin.com.

Mezze, Inc.

Co-founded by Bo Peabody and Nancy Thomas in 2000, and located in the cultural enclave of the Berkshire Hills of Massachusetts, Mezze consists of Mezze Bistro + Bar, its flagship restaurant; Eleven, the restaurant at the Massachusetts Museum of Contemporary Art; and Mezze Catering, a full-service event coordinator. Both Mezze Bistro + Bar and Eleven are Zagat rated.

Village Ventures, Inc.

Co-founded by Matt Harris and Bo Peabody in 2000, Village Ventures is a venture capital firm focused on early-stage investing in emerging geographies across the United States. As its primary source of deal flow, Village Ventures operates a network of early stage venture capital firms with funds in more than a dozen cities. In aggregate, the Village Ventures network manages more than $250 million in assets.

VoodooVox, Inc.

62

Co-founded by Scott Hamilton, Bo Peabody, and Eyal Rimmon in 2000, VoodooVox produces and markets PhoneRescue, a software product that manages the call-in lines of radio and television stations, newspapers, and other media outlets. These customers use PhoneRescue to learn more about their users, advertise to them, and sell them products.

FilmFree Entertainment, Inc.

Co-founded by Joshua Field and Bo Peabody in 2004, FilmFree creates and markets branded DVD movie clubs across different film genres.

Bo Peabody is a well-known entrepreneur. His first company, Tripod, was the eighth largest site on the Internet when it was sold to Lycos in 1998 for $58 million. His second company, Village Ventures, is pioneering new geographic markets for venture capital, managing more than $250 million in several smaller cities across the United States. Bo also co-founded Waterfront Media, Mezze, VoodooVox, and FilmFree Entertainment, four successful (and lucky) start-ups. Bo has been featured in several major media outlets, including *Forbes* magazine, *Fortune* magazine, ABC's *Nightline, BusinessWeek* magazine, *People* magazine, MTV, and *Spin* magazine. He speaks about technology and entrepreneurship at conferences and business schools around the world. Bo lives in New York City and Williamstown, Massachusetts, with his wife, Caroline, who is a fiction writer. He is on the board of the Williamstown Theatre Festival, the Prospect Foundation, and The Academy at Charlemont.

ABOUT THE TYPE

The text of this book is set in a sanserif face called Meta. One of the new modern faces of the past twenty years, it was designed by Erik Spiekermann, Germany's leading graphic designer, and the author of several books on type. Meta was originally conceived for the German subway system but quickly has become one of the most popular typefaces and is often seen in magazines and books. Spiekermann is considered a pioneer type designer. He created the first mail order company for computer fonts and has headed his own graphic design agency, which is a leader in its field, with clients such as Volkswagen, Audi, Apple, and Adobe. His Meta design—along with the other faces he has created such as Officina and Info—has been called the "Helvetica of the nineties."